WHAT BOOKS PRESS

AN IMPRINT OF

THE GLASS TABLE

COLLECTIVE

LOS ANGELES

ALSO BY KEVIN CANTWELL

Something Black in the Green Part of Your Eye

ONE OF THOSE RUSSIAN NOVELS

KEVIN CANTWELL

WHAT BOOKS PRESS

LOS ANGELES

My sincere thanks to the editors who first printed these poems, some in slightly different versions, in the
following publications: "After the Mexican War" in *Alehouse Review*, "The Next Abstinence" in *32 Poems*,
"Canal Boat Portage of the Alleghenies" in *Commonweal*, "Epistle" in *Drunken Boat*, "Last Customer
Played by a Man Called Horse" in *Metre*, "Leslie Norris" in *Poetry Wales*, "Greene County" in *Sentence:
A Journal of Prose Poetics*, "Marlowe in Italy" in *The SHOp*, "Carrabelle River at Dusk" in *South Dakota
Review*, "White Electrical Wire" in *Southern Poetry Review*, "Carpenters at Carrabelle" in *Subtropics*,
and "Dream of a Blue Cloud," "One of Those Russian Novels," and "Night Game Vexed by a Line from
Melville" in *Ninth Letter*.

Thanks especially to Chuck Rosenthal, Gail Wronsky, and to the entire Glass Table Collective. Thanks
to the artist Gronk and to the designer Ashlee Goodwin. And for our happy life, Betsy Lerner.

What Books Press
23371 Mulholland Drive, no. 118
Los Angeles, CA 91364

WHATBOOKSPRESS.COM

Cover art: Gronk, *untitled*, mixed media on paper, 2009
Book design by Ashlee Goodwin, Fleuron Press.

ONE OF THOSE RUSSIAN NOVELS

for

John Caleb Cantwell

CONTENTS

I

The Apple Pipe   15

The Next Abstinence   17

Marlowe in Italy   18

Inviting Some Friends to Supper   21

Greene County   23

Volcanoes Beyond the City   24

Leslie Norris   26

Epistle   27

II

The Wedding Pine   31

Golden Delicious   35

Syllabus & Catechism   38

Last Customer Played by a Man Called Horse   44

III

White Electrical Wire   47

Carrabelle River at Dusk   48

A Puzzle   50

Dobbs Hat   51

Carpenters at Carrabelle   52

Natural History of an Early Winter Drive   53

The Gulf   54

IV

One of Those Russian Novels   57
Speed   59
Beyond Confusion   61
Canal Boat Portage of the Alleghenies   63
After the Mexican War   65
Dream of a Blue Cloud   66
Night Game Vexed by a Line from Melville   67
The Poet at Forty-seven   68

The next morning we were at the mouth of the cave at an early hour, provided with guides, candles and rockets. We explored to a distance of about three miles from the entrance, and found a succession of chambers of great dimensions and of great beauty when lit up with our rockets. Stalactites and stalagmites of all sizes were discovered. Some of the former were many feet in diameter and extended from the ceiling to floor; some of the latter were but a few feet high from the floor; but the formation is going on constantly, and many centuries hence these stalagmites will extend to the ceiling and become complete columns. The stalagmites were all a little concave, and the cavities were filled with water. The water percolates through the roof, a drop at a time—often the drops several minutes apart—and more or less charged with mineral matter. Evaporation goes on slowly, leaving the mineral behind. This in time makes the immense columns, many of them thousands of tons in weight, which serve to support the roofs over the vast chambers. I recollect that at one point in the cave one of these columns is of such huge proportions that there is only a narrow passage left on either side of it. Some of our party became satisfied with their explorations before we had reached the point to which the guides were accustomed to take explorers, and started back without guides. Coming to the large column spoken of, they followed it entirely around, and commenced retracing their steps into the bowels of the mountain, without being aware of the fact. When the rest of us had completed our explorations, we started out with our guides, but had not gone far before we saw the torches of an approaching party. We could not conceive who these could be, for all of us had come in together, and there were none but ourselves at the entrance when we started in. Very soon we found it was our friends. It took them some time to conceive how they had got where they were. They were sure they had kept straight on for the mouth of the cave, and had gone about far enough to have reached it.

Personal Memoirs
Ulysses S. Grant

I

THE APPLE PIPE

a late cousin speaks

Let's walk to this open field where no one
can listen. As that murdered governor was to have said,
     Never write what you can say, never
say what you can imply, nor imply when a wink
     will suffice. Though I stand here
with my thumb cocked & my forefinger straight, do not
     make too much of it when this hammer drops
& a puff of air, which at this distance no one else
     can hear, escapes my pressed lips. Like that girl
who said, slipping in the needle, *like this, like*
     this, *as if it were a pool cue,* you can believe me
now. Coffee is not my first vice, neither my last, but the one
     I begin the day with, the red bridge-light
of the coffee turned on, promising that the buzzing lights
     of the world will be turned on, too. Sometimes
there's cannabis, its dried flower tops broken in the bowl where first
     an apple stem is twisted off, where with one
sharp chopstick a bore is pressed down through the seed-darkened,
     chambered heart, which intersects a slightly
angled second vent, likewise tunneled out by the red & gold
     enameled stick. Hence, a pipe, by which one hit
can be drawn into the lungs, into the black blood,
     the now illuminated day, to soothe the itch, if this be
the bent of need, for methadone, or what has been called
     the chemical life. And driving by, a woman
cannot hide her craving, the glass pipe & a white rock
     & her white face briefly blooming;—but some
wishes, unless spoken, not so obvious, as when
     a happy-looking couple splits up, goes down
respective aisles of their own kinks, she, the spit-
     roasting section, he, where DVDs promise milking mothers,

so that each, strangely partitioned, is just visible
      above the display racks of the mom-and-pop porn emporium,
as in that circle where in stalls or vats or livid clouds
      of wasps, stung by lust or greed, they laugh
in recognition of each other & knowing that this is how,
      at first, they practice happiness.

THE NEXT ABSTINENCE

Tonight, hold that white pill between your teeth—careful
not to place your tongue to it, that first Percocet bitten
    like a cube of sugar some will pour their black tea around.
Let the jar of water wait to be sipped. Let the night lawn whiten with frost.
    Refrain tonight from all you lack. Consider how to do without
another bite—not the pink ribs of a suckling shoat picked to strips;
    nor the last nibbled flesh of a Winesap left so scarce at its core
that the nautilus of its lucent membrane windows the seeds.

Let the last cigarette grow stale; let your memory of it
sweeten. And still gripping that painkiller, bite down to make it half.
    So, if not tonight, & not at once, soon at least, your needs
will grow less incessant of their easy claims: this one tablet, split
    in two, will take you to that one gray hour that is not yet day;
& so, put off the peace it will bring you. Later, take that second half
    at dusk. Break it into twos & those halves then into quarters;
& broken—break *them*, until what you have is a kind of dust
    & then nothing but the stars on sleepless nights
& the moon—full & then its half.

MARLOWE IN ITALY

*[A]bout the tenth hour before noon the afore said
gentlemen met together in a room in the house
of a certain Eleanor Bull, widow...& after
supper the said Ingram & Christopher Morley
were in speech & uttered one to the other divers
malicious words for the reason that they could not
be at one nor agree about the payment of the sum
of pence, that is le recknynge...*

Wm. Danby, Coroner

I

      It is not uncommon to rent a room
like this out back. An old relative,
      dying, could stay here, climb this rise of treads
above the garage, until his few things,
      his hand-saws, his red slippers, his coffee pot,
go on sale on a table in the yard;
      but a boarder such as Marlowe
will ask to use the TR 4, pull off
      its blue plastic tarp, drag it from chokecherry.
And after his errands in town, we'll see him
      wearing a hat woven from yellow grass
as he waters the fruit trees. We'll come home
      one day & he will have knocked down the swifts,
broken honeysuckle from the chimney.

      On one tide the ocean swells; on one
it spills. In one version we will kill a man;
      in one we'll let him live to see his chair
set out in light—but will not see him long,
      a glimpse, to find him on this hill-town path.

In this version, he has slipped from Deptford
          on the outward tide. We see him, therefore,
first in darkness, pricked by briars, designs
          upon his life–pausing–on that boatslip
path, where sodden droops fatten the weeds.

II
          He will take a month to draft a play
or, at this ease, a year; sometimes an act each day;
          but at the time he calls *The End*, Bacon
sits from sleep. We have said his name & leaves
          drop from his hair. Sometimes the weeks slow down,
days interrupted, hours distracted
          by a cart's creaking wheel, its noise coming
closer, rising, not stopping, now going,
          falling, the day tantalized by the approach
of no one who will stop. Where the dead man
          doubles back below on the gravel road,
he's gone to learn his birds, their sketches
          folded as a few signatures into
a chapbook he has then sewn as a guide,
          stitching down the gutter of the pages' crease.
He will end his exile when he can name them
          on the wing or by their bits of shell dropped
through juniper shade as the epistles
          from the Black Sea, the Scythian marshes, rustle
in his hands, & as he soaks his yellow feet
          in the creek-side water of a limestone tub.

III
          Let him live, leaves filling his chair;
have another punk, killed that night, buried instead;
          let Bacon fall back down; allow one S. to perform
with his Players; let the elegies of Ovid,

mailed by the Queen's spy, read as correlative;
have Marlowe touch a lit twig to his *tobacco*;
		let the houseboy of Petro Basconi
bring his letters; have the climate of the south prevail:
		the strange bird-calls at night, the sick odor
of a night-blooming vine; have his mail go
		to Walsingham; let the man who knew
nothing shout *Jesus Christ*! under inquisition.
		Let the houseboy go, weeping.

IV
		And have one live, banished from his City;
let his hair grow to his shoulders, his apartment
		rented to the Irish; have the sun
freckle his fair skin; let him draw up a list
		of Italian phrase-books & histories
numbered with dead kings, requested, sent
		by hand, boat, & mule over a year's time,
finally arriving exactly when his need
		for them is gone; have the olives blacken;
the tiny skeletons, which they will divide
		from the fish, relished; let the convertible
coast down the switchback, its clutch grabbing,
		the ignition failing to start, farther
& farther down, until its rumbling springs
		into its faint motor . . .

INVITING SOME FRIENDS TO SUPPER

But, at our parting, we will be, as when
We innocently met. No simple word,
That shall be uttered at our mirthful board,
Shall make us sad next morning; or affright
The liberty, that we'll enjoy tonight.

Ben Jonson

Each year when the leaves turn red we begin to text
back-and-forth where we'll meet for drinks,
either at the convention's hotel bar or, to avoid
that crowd, some dive five quick minutes away by cab.
And after that din & commotion of whiskeys, neat
or on the rocks, some with just one tiny
splash, a few of us are simply grateful for water,
cold from an iron tap—to have lived, one of us will say, this long
without having killed someone when driving drunk.

Foregoing cabs this time we'll trail back
ten rainy blocks to walk in laughing, as this year again we are the last
to be seated—a long, rowdy table
late to our reservation. And after more drinks, hugs, strange
sudden tears, our menus will be plucked from us
by two waiters annoyed already by the late hour—
& we'll turn to the subject of the war.

We'll thank God that children who are not ours
soldier through those foreign deployments.
We'll console ourselves that on three July days
at Gettysburg—sawed limbs heavy as green wood
after an ice-storm—more died from the shock
of field amputations than have now died

21

in the triangle of death, that blistered Sumerian
watershed. And while we curse the cabinet
that nightly shuffles the cards of those they hate,
we also curse them who have not voted
them out of office. To be sure, there is no
Haldeman or Ehrlichman or Meece
nearby, but we do note the anxious glances
flashed in our direction. Our faces too
are livid, darkened by this hilarity
of wine, yet rigid with the vilifying
jokes we've made of them. Our appetites
have made a mess of this table—bread
broken onto the floor & these quails, half-eaten,
congealed with plums & capers. Like the suitors
Penelope would not join, whose faces were
distended by the equine braying of fear,
nose-blood streaming onto their meats, our faces
will never look so flush.
                                    Our candles burn low.
Our waiter unfolds a tablecloth, crisp as a new flag.
The other diners have stood from their tables,
paid up, disappeared, & our rage has made us
self-conscious. We ask about desert, but decline;
ask for coffee, but sip & let it go cold.
Having said our piece, we sit back. Having kissed
goodbye those we love again even more so than we once did,
we gaze around the table, satisfied
& innocent, each now waiting for a separate cab,
lit from the inside, to pull up outside.
While waiting, we pass around a snifter of brandy so large
it is a glass bowl that a tourist would bring home.
This jar has been sent to our table by the management.
We take their meaning. And yet we linger still & close our eyes
before we sip.

GREENE COUNTY

In this solstice camp, the red spore of reindeer moss rise from the broken
shoulder of the foam target deer—shot through to prove how it can stumble.
Last night, in the yellowing blaze of oaks, I sat up late with my brother,
who spoke of his boyhood friend, adjunct to a general, a major on his way up,
burned alive in September at the Pentagon. Today, my brother's face is mottled
green. He looks to be sleeping, but the grape-whites of his eyes, beneath a net
of camouflage, look elsewhere, not wanting to meet the eye-flicker of a deer,
which say, *Touch Me Not.* He is not the one who's dead, but his face

looks like one I ran a tractor by on a job I'd had. Spraying a hydro-seeder on
a soccer field, the slope adjacent, I coated all of it, a homecoming scarecrow, too,
with the seed glop of glow-green. After a week of rain, two days of sun, a bob
of rye sprouted from its face & from the red flannel wrists that were the nothing
sleeves of straw—

& in a few days the fine grass coarsened & collapsed over the collar, less the
man, more the napping corpse of Whitman's uncut hair. Often you cannot
see—my brother said—a deer approach or hear it step through leaves, nor
know it stands nearby. Call it, one such as this in a garland of red berries,
the cousin to the horse of the Green Knight, its rack a chair of sumac & briar
fronds for legs. I have not said:

We sat under ivied cedar, among the disturbed graves of the family Goss.
I have not said:

We were surrounded by rose & white quartz, the dumb stones of their stillborn
& their slaves. This is where we sit, cold in the sun. This is where we come
when weeping is not enough.

for my brother John
& to the memory of Maj. Cole Hogan,
September 11, 2001

VOLCANOES BEYOND THE CITY

As the small plane banked to land we could see through the window a single
transport lit like a town dropping backward into night where the ocean turned
pink.

And as we drove uphill from Hilo to the national park, Mt. Kea rose behind us
so gradually it might have been the upper pasture of the whitened air.

Signs warned us off beyond the last flow—where it spilled like blackened cake
batter. We would need water, sunscreen, & a hat. And although hikers of all ages
made the trip in a few hours, most returned only after a long day of treading
through the heaps & through the course of those ravines & black moraines.

We paused at a spotting scope, set up to show through the trembling haze how
the lava pulsed.

And then we set off, for a while resolved & talkative, our feet on the crust,
the gritty pastry of that obsidian glaze through which a body might drop
for most of an hour if we ventured upon the dome of that bubble.

You wanted me to tell you about the *Inferno*, but I complained that I was tired,
saying only for a moment midway in the journey of my life I found myself in a
dark wood.

You asked that I go on—but remembering the two lovers, I would not stray
from our happiness to torment you with the empty romance of a few pages;

& then remembering how those two transformed had sounded first like cranes
flying overhead through that polluted mix of hail & cinder & then had perched
to tell their weepy tale, I would not turn to them, nor to the tower of hunger,
nor back to where the poet himself had fainted.

We made our way.

We had seen a couple far behind on the trail, yet now they were ahead on these paths. We had heard her say she'd had enough, that she was turning back, that he could go on; yet, as if she were cold, still she continued on.

We too wanted to reach that spot where, into the South Pacific, the lava flow calved blocks of red glass; & even though we would not reach the place, we kept on because we would never return.

And so we came to that place where we could not go on & where through the seams & fissures, sulfur rushed from vents of heat & made us nearly panic, as if we'd leaned too far over the open flap of an oven door—

the sweets & tripe of our bodies still succulent as we began to burn.

for Betsy

LESLIE NORRIS

What of that Welsh poet who lived south of where I used to live?

What of his pate freckled like a stone tumbled in the gray melt of a river?

What of his two terriers standing beneath a tree on their hind legs nipping sweet peaches despite bees that make them yelp?

What of their red collars hooked on a nail in the garage?

What of him who had mourned a boy from his coal town burned up in the oil smoke of a tank stricken in the Africa campaign against Rommel?

What of his shovels that leaned against the back of the house?

What of his jar of pens?

What of the grass valleys south of the Salt Lake?

Or the white chalk to the west shimmering that was once water?

1921-2006

EPISTLE

I write to remind you that a mourning dove in flight makes the exact sound of a Chevy truck's water-pump pulley about to go, & to say that if that dove were a mimic thrush I would swear that Nature imitated complaint itself.

I write to remind you that the frost on the hood of that truck is shaped exactly like a white moth & that it too goes up into the sun.

We met at a party & you told me the bear poem story you were telling that year: the story from Gary Snyder, who wanted to go bear hunting—said this after some lines on the bear as Native-American spirit wanderer: yet, admits, Snyder,

rube of his own wit, that he wanted to shoot one—then to be told by a man on his logging crew that he couldn't hit—& now I paraphrase—a millpond with a handful of gravel.

We laughed at the story, which I would hear twice more at the same table & at the same bar. You were thirty-five, fifteen years before you would rise from your desk in Richmond, Virginia, struck by how the world was, as never before, so strangely lit.

You stood quickly, as if death were something you forgot to do: a head gate left open & the field poured to stone.

One morning, in the San Joaquin Valley, the ice crown of the Sierras floating in spring over the airborne, glittering dust of the fields, your father had begrudged you permission to bush-hog the grassy aisles between the sapling plums—

& so you slouched in the studied nonchalance of those men who would come up each year from Mexico. You began that day to learn how close you could come and still not get it right, close enough to knock one down, easy as a whipping stick would take the ruby crown from a pokeweed, so that the small tree dropped behind you, dead already, although it would flower before the others, as in the dream of the often-told.

You hoped your father would not notice & so you stabbed it back in, shorter, slightly out of line, planted again until the dried purple leaves fell in the night.

Years later, driving through Peach County, Georgia, you talked about orchards, nights spent out during freezes, lifting the gates of irrigation sloughs to move water through the trees & draw the cold away.

You spoke at length of the two insomniacs of the Civil War, Whitman & Lincoln, walking the summer nights of the capital city.

We agreed that minnows on the rise are goose bumps on the skin. We talked pens, how a nib can tell the left from the right hand & how the poems are in the pen & how you can dip your face to the legal pad & smell the next line.

I have heard that *the pen is the tongue of the hand*.

I saw a man in a Levis jacket on a dirt road. He had a grape knife in his back pocket. He had stopped to toss a dead bird into the grass. This was a dream.

The next morning the first leaves of autumn flecked the cut lawn like rust.

I have been asked if you had children. *Yes. A boy.* What was his name? *Nicholas.* Had I met him? *Once.* The boy had had surgery & his eyes were bandaged, yet he looked up nonetheless. This was not a dream.

You were leading him by the hand, into a building foyer dazzled by its glass— & down the well of iron stairs cold air poured past you.

Larry Levis
1946-1996

II

THE WEDDING PINE

Someone at the party called it a *microburst*, which had made the tree form a cloud of its own destruction from the stillness of an afternoon, so that the massive pine fissured along its entire length & sprang apart in yellow slabs of timbered splints.

The cracking sound, in the single minute of the storm's breakage, reminded the host of wooden grandstands trundling down a street & shattering in the freakish wind of dream.

He repeated what had happened often.

On the day before the party, the one planned down to every detail for the betrothed, as the hostess finished painting the sunroom & as the host thought that he needed to mow the winter yard & while he fished yellow electrical wire from the walls into the dark attic, outside, unbeknownst to him, the sky blackened to a marbled boil of grays.

On an afternoon that had been clear as the face of bone China, it fell in the one place it could have fallen without hitting their house or the neighbor's house or the prized black tupelo or the old stonewall terracing the peach trees.

It fell in the one place it could have fallen. Everyone who saw it at the party agreed. Some took it as prophecy.

The tree was not just any tree but the one left standing when the house was built in the 1930s. Over the years the tree has grown encrusted with disease & a kind of "collarbone" had grown over where a lightening strike had broken it, out of which two parallel yet joined trunks now grew. For a day after it fell, bees walked upon the body of that broken scaffolding, blindly, stiff with cold.

———

One guest had dreamed that very night of an old lover who had locked him from their home & had given away his books & had moved away herself. Yet their house plants remained, withered in the course of a day, & at the kitchen window his avocado plant, its pit in the rusty brine of a Mason jar.

Another guest had also dreamed, but of a wedding where the bride & groom could not break the wine glass wrapped in a napkin & placed on the floor for them to crush. They tried again & again until the father of the groom began to weep.

Yet, one woman at the party insisted that the tree had fallen, it had fallen, she said, in the one place it could fall, in the one place . . .

Another guest, however, remembered a story of a bride thrown from a sled as wolves pursued the newlyweds through a snowstorm that had not let up for a month. It was said that snow fell each year in that forest on that same day, all day, with a fury that locals dreaded, even though they knew it would end, sometimes after a day, sometimes, a week. And although they asked among themselves several times over the years, no one would admit to telling this story. Even though most thought it was the bride's aunt, she denied it; but there were others who believed just as strongly, laughing that people could be so foolishly mistaken, that it had been the date of a distant cousin, a man much older than she.

The trunk stood waist high. Thick limbs were stabbed two feet into the ground. Children from the surrounding houses stood on the barrel of the trunk before the bees made them jump back down.

The point of break was high above the ground & years later the hostess would think of the lone chimney of a burned down house one passes in the country.

———

Despite frightening the young niece who would strew the flowers in a month's time, that same guest went on about the bride thrown from the sled. When the snow came each year as a blizzard on the anniversary of her sacrifice, the husband—for he had not remarried—would not eat & even though he had been forgiven he would not allow himself even the smell of happiness on that day, not the slightest whiff of a roast.

The few foods once brought to him by his father entered a catalogue of dream nausea, which could by mere smell make the voice of his bride tear itself from the clamor of those wolves. So, he sat in the old barn of the family place, deep in the second-growth forest (he had not been able to bring himself to till the land he had been given as a wedding gift), the very barn where one of the horses had died from the exhaustion of terror that long ago night.

The hostess had been right. It had not been an omen of some dark reversal but a prophecy of happiness. With a smile, she reminded everyone at the wedding reception. It had, in fact, fallen in the one place it could have fallen.

The day of the wedding had come. The interior of the old church was laddered with the scaffolding of painters & stained-glass artisans. Although it was a Saturday, one of the craftsmen worked nearly a hundred feet above the guests. Glazing a pane, he worked quietly & slowly, lying on his back on a folded drop cloth. Once, as he paused, he could hear the old monsignor chuckle. The workman was Italian, in this country for the contract of this job. He had been to dozens of weddings & he knew that one of the gags of this happiness had been performed: the best man patting down his pockets, pretending to have lost the rings—or the bride, at the word *obey*, rolling her eyes at the congregation. The old Italian had come to work early & thought he was the only one there, but two women were there, late in middle-age, yet still very beautiful. As he lifted his buckets of tools from the van, he understood from their conversation that they were waiting for the florist & as he stood near them for a moment, unlocking a side door, one of them spoke of having fresh snow sprinkled on summer grapes when she was a child, before the revolution, in the mountains of Iran.

And as he climbed the tiers of the construction braces, pulling his buckets behind him with a short piece of rope, one level to another, sometimes pressing the heaviest of the two over his head like a weightlifter, he thought of when he was a young man, how he would have painted a still-life of such grapes & what he would have written instead of his signature, in the flourish of his youth, as a small phrase of allegory, something to annoy his old teacher, something about confectioner's sugar on the lips of the Beloved.

for my brother Terry

GOLDEN DELICIOUS

We are driving to the border, toward the western
Alabama hills of Georgia, the last rolling
remnants of the Lookout Mountain escarpment.
We are talking horses & slowing down
to look at ponies, the days after Christmas
lazy & warm—my son, my wife, her mother
enjoying the drive, the end of the year.
She is an old woman now, eighty-seven,
riding with the window open, the breeze
in her hair, which she has let down & let
grow long, white as a seed-pod burst
in the day's heat, her hair
long as Lyndon Johnson's, lanky & white
with his suffering, which would not end the war,
nor slow the hill-country sun from falling. She
will not die of grief, although it will be her heart
someday, & her white spitz Snowflake
will lie down & not leave her body.

                                   Her mother
had ponies before she was born, but she
died young & Mary did not get to see
her mother ride. For a few miles more we are quiet,
& I remember years ago in the Wind Rivers
when the horses were let out at dusk,
more than a hundred of them, hungry
enough I was told that they would not
run far. When she was young her father
gave them whiskey to help them sleep
when they were ill, opened the windows to the winter
nights, but her room was on the other side
of the house from the lake & so

it wasn't that bad. When she was a newlywed
during the war, Mary rode horses
out of Army stables kept for the wives of officers.
She had jodhpurs, black boots, & a white silk scarf.

Sometimes she doesn't know
her son's first wife from his second,
his children from the marriage
that went bad or those from the one
that did not. She laughs.
When her doctor asked her to subtract
seven from a hundred she could not
think & for a joke this beautiful afternoon

we ask if she knows the name
of the idiot president, the five Texas rivers
that run southeast to the sea, if she knows
her own name, how much is twelve
times thirteen. She was a trained physician
once, quick with numbers & all those parts
of the body—but wanted instead to raise a family.

A day later
so much of this happiness has wearied
into the anxieties of next year & her house is still
in disrepair. The plants inside
press to the window for light,
her once fine yard grown to sapling brambles where anyone
might park a tractor for good until they were
too old to leave the house. Her pitted tree
holds a few yellow apples. At the steps outside
she grips a paper bag of her presents,
new slippers & bath oils & her small, black umbrella
she uses these days for a cane.
We don't think her furnace has worked in years,
but it is her house she often tells us & she will not

let us come in—yet the large black dog
she took in as a stray, rescued from rain
she says was *terrible, terrible,*
left inside overnight to chase the mice around,
now leaps with happiness at her voice.

SYLLABUS & CATECHISM

If you have a family emergency, call 911.

———

Because my name is at the top of the syllabus. That's why.

———

If I wanted your opinion, I would take a class from you.

———

If you believe, as you say you do, that some things *are* a matter of opinion,
you are correct; but it's my opinion that counts.

———

Does the umpire argue balls & strikes?

Does the umpire ask the man in the bleachers if the glove at second-base
was put down?

Except for his dark collar, does the umpire look like a Jesuit?

Except for my dark collar, do I look like a Jesuit?

Do I want to chop logic?

I do not.

Will I argue with you about what time the sun comes up?

I will not.

I will, however, provide you with a note to the clerk of the municipal court, with whom you can render, at length, your disposition.

———

How should you end your paper? (Now we are getting somewhere.)

With a period.

———

If you sleep in my class even once, I will drop you like a red brick in the green ocean.

If your breathing sounds like snoring & your eyes are closed, don't do that either.

———

If you want to hope & pray, feel free; but you might try cracking the book.

Have I read the Bible? I have indeed, in particular, Isaiah, who saith
Your ass is grass.

———

If you have poems you wish for me to read, burn them, wet your finger in their
    ashes, brush the sign of the cross on your forehead & keep moving.

No. I do not want to hear your dream.

No. You may not use my office phone.

No. I do not have an extra pen.

No. I did not read your email.

Yes. I saw that you sent it, but no I did not read it.

No. I will not read it. But you may print it out & use my Zippo to make it
    burn in your hand & therefore provide its own light.

———

Who is the Ancient Mariner? Short-stop for the '79 Braves, *who stoppeth one of three.*

How does *Moby Dick* end? With a period.

———

"To action Oedipus is never late,
While Hamlet forever vacillates."

Discuss. Double space. Write in ink. Number your pages. There is no need for a title. You have one hour.

———

If your spelling is Elizabethan, *Webster's New Collegiate Dictionary* will help.

———

Will I write you a letter of recommendation?

Yes, but remind me of your name.

　　To whom it may concern:

　　According to my records, so-and-so was a student in my class in _____.
　　He/she earned a/an _____ in said class.

　　I have heard from a reliable source that his/her car/truck/bicycle is
　　now operating on a regular basis. I remember that his/her phone
　　was always reliable.

　　　　　　　　　　　　　　　　　　Yours sincerely,
　　　　　　　　　　　　　　　　　　Instructor of Record

Will this do or shall I make something up?

　　　　　　　　　　　———

Speak up, son. The worst that can happen? Strangers will turn in their seats to
laugh at you.

　　　　　　　　　　　———

I am sorry but you will hate me longer than I will remember your name & that
one month, one day, a minute after you die, even those who love you will forget
to think of you, like the boy Scotty in that story, whose cake with his name
sits on a bakery shelf midweek after he's died.

　　　　　　　　　　　———

No, no. I will remember your face, regardless of how it has altered, but not whether I passed you up to the next wit.

———

Unless, as these barbarians will do, your body has fallen into the kindling of a pyre, the mower at the city cemetery will clip your headstone as it makes the turn.

———

Rumi says that if you want something, want it for yourself.

———

Even Saint Augustine, when turning to God, had to ignore his child plucking the hem of his clothing.

———

If you need this class to graduate, keep that fact in front of you at all times.

———

If you want an A, you make it on the last day, at the buzzer, with a hand in your face, a three-pointer from downtown.

———

If you get behind, don't worry. We offer this class next semester, too.

for Seamus Deane

LAST CUSTOMER PLAYED
BY A MAN CALLED HORSE

This day—& its beaten leaves, & these yellow five-fingered
sweetgum hands, down; & these blood-red tupelos, tear-dropped

& down. I'm finished with *This Sporting Life* & the man called horse has left
his red face at the bar & will now have nothing not the Dickel not the Beam

—but tea with lemon & a sugared spoon, & the *Times* of London
& the *New York Times*, spread on the floor, the flags, the quarry-cold, the riven

slates & at his elbow, cold cuts if his hunger comes to that—*Thrift, thrift,*
Horatio! The funeral bake-meats did coldly furnish forth the marriage tables...

That's Richard Harris complaining that he would have made a good Hamlet.
The year—done, & the hour of his idling hearse ends in its yard. In that bistro,

twenty years ago, the red leaves skittered in. His bill, unsettled; his, the last
table; me, his waiter in the wicket of traffic passing in both directions; rain

freckling the papers I'd gone to fetch for him. Last night, the folio scent,
the Avon pulp of that paperback Storey book pressed to my face.

His wishes, the same: a good obituary, a cigarette, the sun on his bare feet.

R.H.
1930-2002

III

WHITE ELECTRICAL WIRE

One winter, during the afternoons after work,
Saturdays & on a few Sundays, I pulled wire
through the walls of an outbuilding tool room.
Up & down an aluminum ladder, one day,
tired, in a hurry before I lost the sun, I nearly
electrocuted myself, pulling on
a rotten cloth-insulated feeder, the thick sparks
popping in the dusk of the attic.
Prone across joists, alive, I watched wasps
sucked out through the slats of louvered light.

For years I was used to that darkness, forgetting
the switch-box I'd installed, having to open
both doors of the tool room to find poisons,
saws, the 90- and 40-weights, the 2-cycle oils,
the drive-belts polished beyond use, a basket
of work-gloves, stiff as seed pods, dry as leaves;
the mauls, the wedges, & the Nicholson files;
the bearings punched out of axles, the nicked
mower blades, the squat plugs of trucks long since
sold, & the extension ladder my father used
for thirty years, on which I had climbed that day
into a draft of rising dust, & then down, taking back
each step, carrying the weight of this life
that still I could not part with, not its levers, nor
its pulleys, not the jar, not the wick, not the oil.

CARRABELLE RIVER AT DUSK

This near the ocean one cannot tell,
if not from these parts,

whether the sea falls unseen & crumbles
to the left or swells

to the right & rises beyond this grass
whitened by the sun. Do not ask

a local fisherman on this public dock—
for he may not look at you at all but at the sun

instead & someone who feels sorry for you
will say, *The tide is coming in—*.

For some that says too much.

Across the river now that night has come
welders in their sputtering pauses

illuminate the pitch of a steel barge

& yet, one cannot hear them speak
if they speak at all,

nor hear any sound if there is a sound;
neither the slap of water nor a mosquito

slapped; neither the rasp of a lighter
nor laughter, if they laugh—

only what can be known; from here,
what can be seen,

& if not seen, what must be believed,
even in darkness-

the nickel pastures of the sea.

A PUZZLE

emphysema

I draw a red arrow counterclockwise
        on a piece of masking tape. "Turn it left,
for ON." She understands, but then—bereft,
        each breath comes out squeezed.
The oxygen tank's valve confuses her.
        I show her on the green spare, ON, then OFF—
at first the rushing hiss, the breathless air,
        & then the needle bobbing on what's left.

DOBBS HAT

My father had seen the Tigers play in Detroit one day
& Trevino, the next, a real scorcher, too; & sick

already he'd bought the hat, crisp as an Easter basket.
He was up there seeing his three brothers for the last time

more than a decade ago. Unkempt itself
these days, it's a Panama of whitened grass.

I wear it cutting brush in Florida,
in yellow flies & the dropping ash of burning vines.

CARPENTERS AT CARRABELLE

after Ralph Thompson

Mister Johnstono, union carpenter moonlighting
on sick-pay, snaps the chalk line like a bra-strap
      & straight as a shore leaves a blue line across
the cement block wall of an outbuilding. His granddaughter
      Xaviéra rips nailers from bald-cypress planks
scavenged from an ice-house on the Wacissa River.
      As she bends to the cut, around her white waist & hips
across the small of her back loops the Gothic ink
      of a diamond snake & though it tightens its grip it does not
move above the top of her jeans.
                  The corner posts of the bump-out
shed *thrum* in the hardened concrete. We test them
      like bowstrings. We wait for the truck with the roofing,
corrugated like a plowed tin field. She says each panel
      could fly up, each piece in a gust of leaves. This—
a story from television: Sailors said the Magnetic Islands would pull
      nails from passing frigates. Instead, we see a bungalow
on the state highway, a house where there was no house,
      on the sagging beds of tandem trailers, hogging both lanes.
A grown boy rides the roof-wobble of that creaking rig,
      as if flood has forced him there in the yellow-fly dusk
—the high road-side pines like grass divided & the black
      slough of tar winding into the ocean of night.

NATURAL HISTORY OF AN EARLY WINTER DRIVE

At twilight, the old snow of cotton in the remnant furrows.

———

Whenever I pass the sign *8 Miles*
to Ochlocknee
there is that poet from there I remember
at a party in a forest-green apartment
looking out on the East River
saying he wished there was more bread

———

& Muldoon, ruminating on his puns & funny words,
who'd asked about *Fat Lighter*
in white letters on the drop-gate of a black truck

———

& Swift, fashioning a game-snare
he called a *springe*
from a plum switch & the wiry hair

———

of a Yahoo but night—
its toils & deep in its first hour a fat doe
hangs from a swing set,
the night-blooming flower of its gut opened in the porch light.

THE GULF

At Carrabelle they throw their trash,
their oyster shells shucked on holidays,
        all that their hands touch in a day,
into the weeds & the roadside grass.

        At first I picked it up and swore,
foil, boxes, cigarettes, their oil quarts,
        before I'd cut the yard in shorts
and flip-flops from a dollar store.

Comes a week, though, a month, a year
        of illness elsewhere—a string of frazzled
Christmas lights, vine through a dazzle
        of morning glory, would appear.

Years—I burned it all in a pit,
        raked its whitened ash and oily billow
where purslane spreads its surf—but now
        I just run the mower over it:

leaves & paper chopped up with grass.
        Cups mildew where the mulcher cannot reach.
And past the collapsed oaks—the beach,
        where surf compounds its bits of glass.

for Dan & Monica

IV

ONE OF THOSE RUSSIAN NOVELS

Sumatra, Florida

On a chalk road north of Sumatra,
we drove inland from the ocean's light.
The leaves were paper; rain, the gray light
of stars on a white-grass river.

We drove inland from the ocean's light;
we drove from the flat sea, past a house—
past rain-stars on a white-grass river,
the house set back in tents of hemlock.

We drove from the gray sea, past a house
run with water streaks, two stories up,
set back in rain, in tents of hemlock
& stands of palmetto, stands of pine.

Run with droops of moss, two stories up,
as in one of those Russian novels,
but here in palmetto; here, in pine—
a house, a room, a man by himself.

As in one of those Russian novels,
but here—eating his chocolate cake,
a room at dusk, a man by himself
whose son will not come to the table.

Here, a man eating chocolate cake,
on his son's birthday, whose mother weeps,
& who will not come to the table,
who sits on a couch in the ruined trees.

On his birthday the boy's mother weeps
& hears rain & a car going by,
& sits on a couch in the ruined trees
& hears a man weep at a table,

who hears the rain, a car going by
through paper leaves, rain made of gray light—
& hears himself weep at a table
near a chalk road north of Sumatra.

SPEED

Pindaric with lines from Yogi Berra

slows the game down; the pitcher
steps off; the runner, back; the throw to first;
  the pitcher, on; his wind-up; the runner, off.
    The distance between the batter's box
& first base is the same as between the first
  stress of pentameter & the last—anything more
  & there's no game; less, & a catcher,
one of those guys who will spend the season halfway
    through Camus, & slow as an ice wagon,
could walk there & turn left.

———

    Each stadium has its own porch,
its own dimensions, its corners & caroms,
  its tricks of wind & where *it gets late early*
the way the sun drops behind the lights
    —or the way that a single on Astroturf
will run on you, or how a double
  can die as a single in the long grass of that stanza
  by Whitman, where the game is two words, a gap
between, through which Kenny Lofton can triple.

———

    There is no sweeter laugh than at Wrigley,
a day game in September, *where if you weren't*
  awake, you'd still be sleeping, where Mickey Hatcher
    tears at the ivy looking for the ball;
no colder evening than at Candlestick,
  the ocean fog spilling over

the rim of the bleachers, Willie Mays
blowing into his hands; & no slower motion
than a ball up the chimney...

———

Although they do hear music
no one else hears, the horse-clatter of claves
twitching their limbs, the Fungo Kings are not
a marimba and steel-drum section
but the grapefruit-league coaches,
the Latin baseball men who point to their heads,
saying that the ball is round
but it comes in a square box.

BEYOND CONFUSION

At Point-of-the-Mountain Prison, Hoffman,
the "Mormon Bomber," balanced the trigger's bleb,
the mercury bubble of his device,
trembling now even as he made it again
in memory—hoping it would not take
his fingers off. His cell was in another
wing, where he, ingenious in his sin,
bunked alone. On the steep grade outside
the yard, idling diesels, frozen in black tarps,
throbbed on winter nights, waiting for the snow
to end. Even then, for a nothing kind
of pay, I taught a class a week. They let me in
one gate—unchained!—before I walked along
a wall of handball games, interrupting them
who stood back for a moment while I passed.
I would then climb a tunnel of stairs
to a room, where they sat in the dark blue
coats of the State & took down notes, although
I would not proctor a test nor correct
papers, nothing but a weekly talk—
on Whitman first, at whose name they had smirked
because they knew the kind of man he'd been.
Dickinson they knew from Hoffman's forgeries.
This got them on how they could be released,
set loose from school with such a note, in name
only by their mothers—let out one day
one of them said to swim a county river,
the water swift with spring & gravelly melt.
One night on Frost one stood mid-poem as I read,
witnessing the life he'd had, who said That
was my house *a house in earnest*. He sat

again. He stood. He sat. One of his friends
tried to laugh this off—as if to mean This
idiot here you cannot bring him anywhere,
not *church*, not *here*, without him counting up
his dogs by name & then gaping around
in tears, or numbering apples from his father's trees—
as if *they* could be put back, made whole again.

CANAL BOAT PORTAGE OF THE ALLEGHENIES

U. S. Grant, 17 yrs. old, on his way to West Point

In this heat the sunflowers cannot lift their heads
nor the mockingbird

cease, but the canal rises, each section
more shallow, each part once a river now a pool,

rockier, more sky than deep
water—until they must winch the boat, the sodden keel

plowing a black wave of earth,
its timber nearly

breaking over the last stone rib of the crest.

———

There is that mare he walks beside
who speaks to him of carrots & oats

taken from his clean hand.

On the watershed he steps
her back in her traces, until the sisal hums,

lowering the boat down.

———

A week later, he cannot count the lamps
& tar pots that burn

all night on the scaffolds of the East River,
nor the thousands who work on the glittering risers

of that ship they will cross on.

AFTER THE MEXICAN WAR

Bluecoats, shavetails, they are not
the accidentals birders list as such if winds have taken them
        elsewhere, but Union officers. Ulysses Grant
is one & all climb the white-washed snow of Popocatépetl.
        In a few years a rebel, Anderson will hold
for an afternoon the one road into Spotsylvania.
        On this day south of Cholula, storms keep them
from the volcano summit, forcing them down,
        hip-deep in slush, through cloud & white sun.

Snowblind for a few days they fret
aloud that their eyes will go soft as old plums,
        & will never clear up, like a spotting scope
for a Howitzer dropped, the prism inside
        jostled askew, so that the lens can never
squint up a landscape again, no matter
        how they blink.

Their horses, hungry where they are tethered,
rear back from these bandaged faces, pulling
        their bridles against the buck-toothed jars
of their own thick skulls; yet these bays & sorrels know
        these voices soon & these hands upon them,
which will lead them down to the river,
        though these soldiers are blind, & then uphill
through pines, in darkness, though in this dream
        they believe it is light.

.

DREAM OF A BLUE CLOUD

In those first books of early mountaineering literature,
they were smokers—old briars & the new cigarettes. They were third sons,
holiday amateurs, captains; they were keen mechanics
of their iron tanks, their adjustable spanners, & their breathing hoses.
Some believed that the deep inhalation of the blue cloud
helped them oxygenate the blood, the secret capillary branches of the lungs
pulsing with light, deciduous then fading. They smoked outside
in the chill night & in the poor neighborhoods of the high camps.
And on a housekeeping day, after a storm, they broke
their paperbacks down the spine, like bread divided, one man reading
chapter one, the other, denouement, their clothes drying
on the talus, an alcohol stove wheezing in the altitude, the brass hookahs
bubbling in Conan-Doyle—crumbled grains of hash & opium
tar, the bellows of their lungs ballooning, the streams of smoke
expelled, their eyes opening, half closing; someone
who would call them, yet who could not be seen; someone they would call
& call, yet who would not wake: the prayer flags above them
as pennants of ice-crystal, the streams of alto-cirrus,
as mares'-tails, as nightmares . . .

NIGHT GAME VEXED BY A LINE FROM MELVILLE

Moth-time, midsummer, the bedroom in the dark.
        For a while out west in Oakland, the blue lid of twilight

fluttered over the stadium like the milk eye of the world
        putting off sleep. For a moment the game was a base-hit

from done. Now, too lonely to stand, a few fans
        wait out the extra-innings into the early morning—

the length of a night-shift & then never going home.
        In the breath it would take to unfold the fan of a newspaper,

the centerfielder turns to go back for something.
        Even on the radio I can hear him call for it

in that shell of sleep—& Melville himself, restless
        with the voices on the wind, a crowd & its *mixed surf*

of *muffled sound* from his house-top room—
        the draft riot in Lower Manhattan late in the war.

THE POET AT FORTY-SEVEN

Because I have let this page yellow
& my black hair gray, because each night the dipper of stars
        ladles deeper into the stream, & because
I am nearly fifty-one, it is time to quit dragging my feet,
        fixed to my reflection in the blotched, hallway glass.
Too old to be a young poet, still I am young enough
        to have lost a Congressional election, my half-life
ahead of me; old enough to be mistaken
        for my father as he comes down the stairs
past midnight, clown-faced with insomnia,
        yet too young to pay an older man to climb
the tensile dip of an extension ladder & chip
        paint from the white weatherboards of this house
& fend the sleepy bats that crease the light
        & loop below the eaves. I can remember
the woods pooled in dusk, fireflies
        on & off, tricked by a lighter I flicked on
& off, that same year I stood at a Dead concert,
        a fool like anyone else. I have learned
an easy anecdote for one of those pauses
        at a summer party, the one I tell about Gore
Vidal, some kind of cousin to the once
        Vice President. The cousin, having been asked
if he would like to meet his distant kinsman,
        said, No, that he had met altogether too many
Vice Presidents. I myself have met altogether
        too many poets. So give me a chair of planks
set back beneath the shade of a fig, a pistol
        to wave at trespassing children, a bitter fice to flush
the proselytizers off my porch, & the *Times*
        fat with obituaries. Give me a jar of water

& the last cigarette of the day. Who would not
         crave this private life? How could anyone not
ask for mercy from these poets, dressed like
         the friends of Emerson, yet with apple-green
loafers, each with a physique lean from spinning
         & pilates? Give me, my friend, that wild hog instead,
which had feasted, crushing the leaves of oaks—
         shot with a glass arrow from a tree-stand, cooked
in a pit, under corn shucks & a rain-soaked tarp.
         Bring me a sheaf of Blue Horse notebook paper,
which I can fill with more complaints, while on
         this small radio a hard ball skips through the gap,
the announcer saying we can close the book
         on this game, though the switched-off dial turns on
the ravenous static of these insects,
         but cannot stop the gear of that oil-well, which would lift & drop
all night when I was a child, pulling from the vast
         middle reaches of that black lake below, a tipping
swell on its bubble, though now it is this sweet ink
         & a sketch of a mockingbird.

NOTES

A line in "Epistle" is from Warren Chappell, *A Short History of the Printed Word*, Hartley & Marks Publishing, 2000.

Ulysses S. Grant, *Personal Memoirs*, ed. Caleb Carr, Random House/Modern Library, 1999.

The epigraph from "Inviting Some Friends to Supper" comes from a poem of similar title in *Ben Jonson: The Complete Poems*, ed. George Parfitt, Yale University Press, 1982 (1975).

Lines in "Syllabus & Catechism" are owed to Seamus Deane, *Reading in the Dark*, Knopf, 1997.

A line in "Beyond Confusion" is from *The Poetry of Robert Frost*, Holt, Rinehart and Winston, 1969.

Some images and a brief passage in "Marlowe in Italy" are based on Charles Nicholl, *The Reckoning*, University of Chicago Press, 1992.

KEVIN CANTWELL is the author of *Something Black in the Green Part of Your Eye* (New Issues) and editor of a chapbook series for Georgia poets who have not published a first book. He lives in Macon, Georgia, with his wife Betsy Lerner. His poems have appeared in *Antioch Review, Commonweal, Metre, The New Republic, Paris Review, Poetry, Poetry Wales, The SHOp, Southwest Review,* as well as other magazines.

Printed in the United States
148735LV00001B/6/P